IMAGES
of America

IDAHO STATE PARKS

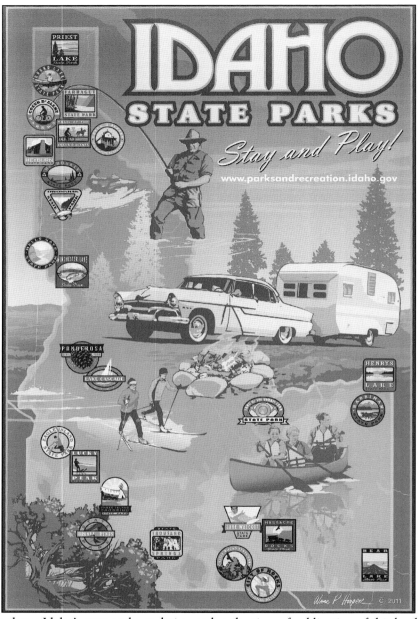

This map shows Idaho's state parks as designated at the time of publication of this book. Thirty parks are included, though many people think of the satellite units of Thousand Springs State Park, Niagara Springs, Crystal Springs, Box Canyon, Billingsley Creek, Ritter Island, and Malad Gorge as state parks. As you shall see, there has never been total agreement in Idaho about what is a state park and what is not. (Courtesy Idaho Department of Parks and Recreation.)

ON THE COVER: Swimmers and boaters are on Payette Lake around 1910. (Courtesy Idaho State Historical Society 3781.)

IMAGES
of America

IDAHO STATE PARKS

Rick Just
Foreword by Gov. Cecil D. Andrus

ARCADIA
PUBLISHING

Published by Arcadia Publishing
Charleston, South Carolina

Printed in the United States of America

Library of Congress Control Number: 2016959656

For all general information, please contact Arcadia Publishing:
Telephone 843-853-2070
Fax 843-853-0044
E-mail sales@arcadiapublishing.com
For customer service and orders:
Toll-Free 1-888-313-2665

Visit us on the Internet at www.arcadiapublishing.com

To Gov. Robert E. Smylie, the father of Idaho's state parks, and Yvonne S. Ferrell, whose leadership is still felt in the state parks system

CONTENTS

FOREWORD

In a state with such stunning beauty it might seem obvious that Idaho should set aside land for the enjoyment of our citizens and vacationing visitors. Yet it took nearly 50 years from the creation of Idaho's first state park to organize an agency of professionals to run a statewide system of parks. This was probably because of an abundance of riches. Idaho's public lands, managed mostly by the federal government, were so readily accessible for outdoor recreation that to some it seemed like a duplication of effort to provide even more opportunity.

The federal government did not have all of Idaho's natural resources, though. They did not have the best white sand beaches on Priest Lake, Millionaire's Hole at Harriman State Park, or that peninsula in Payette Lake, now known as Ponderosa State Park. Nor did they have cultural resources such as the Cataldo Mission or the ghost town of Bayhorse.

Idaho citizens needed places where they could picnic, hike, and boat near where they lived. They wanted safe places where they could teach their kids to camp and fish that were close to home.

I have been a supporter of Idaho's state parks since the beginning. I was a senator in the Idaho Legislature when we passed then governor Robert Smylie's bill to create what is today the Idaho Department of Parks and Recreation. It was one of Governor Smylie's finest acts.

We treasure our federal lands in Idaho, from the Frank Church River of No Return Wilderness to the vast sagebrush steppe along the Snake River Plain. Those lands call to hardy adventurers of every kind. Yet we also need nearby state parks where people who cannot adventure as much as they used to can still enjoy the great outdoors, and where those just learning to adventure can whet their appetite for the future.

This book tells the colorful history of Idaho's state parks, and it will help you love them even more. Enjoy.

Warmest regards,
Cecil D. Andrus
Former Governor of Idaho

ACKNOWLEDGMENTS

I wish to thank Cecil D. Andrus, former Idaho governor and secretary of the interior whose vision and leadership in both roles was so important for parks and public lands in the United States, for his thoughtful foreword to this book. For their parts in providing the historical photographs that made this book possible, I thank Jennifer Okerlund, Jan Boles, Dennis Woolford, Kevin Lynott, John Sullivan, Kyle Babbit, Leo Hennessey, Charlie Chase, Mary McGraw, Tabitha Erday, and Jim Duran. For clarification on property size and ownership issues, thanks go to Jeff Cook and Connie Vaughn. Thanks are extended to David Langhorst, the current director of the Idaho Department of Parks and Recreation, for his support of this project and especially to Bob Meinen, twice director, who gave me the latitude to become the unofficial historian of the parks system.

Unless otherwise credited, all photographs are courtesy of the Idaho Department of Parks and Recreation. In photograph credit lines, ISHS stands for the Idaho State Historical Society and LC stands for the Library of Congress.

INTRODUCTION

Idaho has gorgeous parks any state would be proud to claim. Yet state leaders were often reluctant to create a state park or even to accept the donation of one. It was 57 years after property for the first state park was acquired before an agency was created to manage Idaho's parks.

Over those decades, parks came and went, some managed by the Idaho Department of Lands, some by Fish and Game, some by Public Works, and still others by the Idaho Department of Transportation. Properties under the designation "state park" ranged from half-acre roadside rest areas with a picnic table to the spectacular Shoshone Falls.

One park in particular seemed by its name to recognize the rarity of state parks in Idaho. A five-acre site along the Boise River just downstream from Lucky Peak Dam was acquired by the state in 1935. It was a popular site for picnicking in the 1930s, 1940s, and 1950s, getting many mentions in newspaper articles about social gatherings. It was called simply State Park.

Robert E. Smylie, who became governor in 1955, wanted to elevate the status of state parks in Idaho by creating a professional agency to manage them. He proposed a state parks department three times before the Idaho Legislature finally relented on his fourth proposal and created the Idaho Department of Parks in 1965. It would later become the Idaho Department of Parks and Recreation (IDPR).

It was a major donation from the Harriman family that changed those legislative minds.

The governor had known E. Roland Harriman for some time when, in 1959, Harriman called to talk about the donation. Harriman and his brother Averell wanted to see the 11,000-acre Railroad Ranch they owned protected from development, in the tradition of their father, E.H. Harriman, who had purchased land along the Hudson River in New York bit by bit for preservation. After his death, Mary Harriman donated the 20,000 acres her husband acquired to the State of New York, making it a central part of Palisades Interstate Park. That donation is why Idaho's park is called Harriman State Park of Idaho, to distinguish it from the older Harriman State Park of New York.

Governor Smylie saw the potential donation of the Railroad Ranch as his chance to get a park system in place. Working mostly with Roland Harriman, the majority owner of the property, Smylie inserted language in the gift deed that Idaho must have a professionally trained park service before the transfer of the property could be made.

Negotiations of this sort need to happen in private so that news accounts do not risk blowing the agreement before all parties are ready to sign. The *Idaho Statesman*, the state's leading newspaper, had criticized the governor's frequent trips out of state and particularly the apparent secrecy of one he took to New York in December 1961. But when Smylie announced the donation of the Railroad Ranch on December 22, those concerns seemed to vanish.

Meanwhile, a transfer of land from the federal government that had been in the works since 1948 was about to take place. The old Farragut Naval Training Station, which briefly became Farragut College from 1946 to 1949, had long since been decommissioned. The Idaho Land Board, led by the governor, agreed to a swap of state land along the North Fork of the Clearwater River that was set to be inundated by construction of the Dworshak Dam, for the old naval base.

Smylie envisioned Farragut as the northern anchor of a string of parks extending south and east to the Railroad Ranch property near the Wyoming border. If he could show the legislature the economic benefit of state parks, he might be able to get his park system.

That economic benefit came dressed in skirts and shoulder sashes. Governor Smylie negotiated successfully with the Girl Scouts to hold a large national encampment at Farragut in 1965. At about the same time, he started what would be successful talks with the Boy Scouts, hoping to win the organization's approval for Farragut as the site of the 1967 World Scout Jamboree.

For the 1965 legislative session, Smylie had a state park with a mission, Farragut, and a jewel of a park in the wings in the form of the Railroad Ranch. Further, he had the advantage of a newly minted federal program, today called the Land and Water Conservation Fund (LWCF), that would provide substantial capital for development of a new park system.

Political observers look at the 1965 Idaho Legislature as one of the most important in the state's history. Smylie finally got his parks department that year. Some say the establishment of the merit-based Idaho personnel system in 1965 was nudged along by the clause Smylie had inserted in the Harriman gift deed that specified an agency of park professionals be in place before the Railroad Ranch would become the property of the state. That legislative session saw the establishment of a state personnel retirement system and, most importantly, the institution of a 3¢ sales tax.

Governor Smylie had worked tirelessly for those measures, many of which were unpopular with the conservative wing of the Republican Party. One of those conservatives was Don Samuelson, a state senator for whom Smylie had campaigned in 1960. The progressive turn of the 1965 legislature was too much for some in the Republican Party, who put Samuelson up as a primary opponent to the three-term governor. Smylie did not take the upstart opponent seriously. He underestimated some of the seething opposition in his own party to the new sales tax and paid little attention to his own reelection. As a result, Samuelson rolled over Smylie, taking 40 of 44 counties in the primary. That the governor got credit or blame for the tax was apparent in stores around the state where patrons ponying up those extra pennies grumbled about paying "Smylie money." No other politician who had supported the tax was defeated that election and the sales tax is today a crucial component of Idaho's budget.

For his tireless efforts on behalf of state parks, Smylie, who died in 2004, is remembered as the father of Idaho's state park system. The administrative headquarters for IDPR is housed today in the Robert E. Smylie Building in Boise.

One

Heyburn, the Pacific Northwest's First State Park

In 1908, the US Congress set aside 5,500 acres of land and water near St. Maries for the State of Idaho to use as a park. US senator Weldon B. Heyburn had introduced a bill to make the land a national park. Heyburn was an adamant foe of public lands and fought vehemently against every wish of the newly formed US Forest Service and its head, Gifford Pinchot. Yet Heyburn did see the value of designating a national park in his home state.

The US Senate passed Heyburn's bill, but it did not survive negotiations in the House of Representatives. Ultimately, Congress passed a bill allowing the State of Idaho to purchase the land, which had formerly been a part of the Coeur d'Alene Indian Reservation, which was being terminated. Every Coeur d'Alene tribal member would get 160 acres. The rest, minus the park, would be sold to the public. It was not until 1911 that the State of Idaho actually got around to purchasing the land from the federal government, for $15,000, using timber taken from the new park as a source for part of the payment.

The Idaho Legislature voted to name the new park after Senator Heyburn, who died in 1912. Mount Heyburn in the Sawtooth Range and the city of Heyburn both bear the senator's name. That two significant public land sites bear the name of a public land foe is galling to some in the conservation community. When Timothy Eagan's popular book *The Big Burn* came out in 2009, reminding readers of Heyburn's fights with the US Forest Service and allegiance to land barons, IDPR received several suggestions that the name of the park be changed. There was not enough steam behind the idea to move it forward.

US senator Weldon B. Heyburn was a staunch opponent of federal lands. Nevertheless, he wanted one national park in Idaho. He fought against the idea of making that site a state park because, as he said, state parks "are always a subject of political embarrassment." That the property he championed as a national park actually became Idaho's first state park in 1908 and that the Idaho Legislature named it after the senator must have given him conflicting emotions. (Courtesy LC-DIG-hec-15308.)

Prior to installation of the Post Falls Dam in 1908, Hidden, Round, Benewah, and Chatcolet were individual lakes, except during high water when they merged with the larger Lake Coeur d'Alene. The dam holds the lake at its high-water level, so the St. Joe River, which winds between the southern lakes, has now all but disappeared, leaving just a thin strip of bank on either side through Heyburn State Park. (Courtesy ISHS 60-173.33.)

Two

THE CONSERVATION CONSCIENCE OF E.H. HARRIMAN

Edward Henry Harriman, who went by E.H., ran Union Pacific Railroad. He was not a typical railroad baron at the turn of the 20th century. He had a deep appreciation for nature and a philanthropic bent. Harriman was an outdoorsman who was involved in the early conservation movement. He was friends with John Muir and had supported Muir's efforts to keep a dam from being built in Yosemite's Hetch Hetchy Valley.

In 1899, his doctors advised Harriman to take a break from his hectic life and get a little rest. Harriman thought going to Alaska to hunt bears would do the trick. Since he was going anyway, why not take a few friends?

The steamship *George W. Elder* sailed from Seattle on May 31, 1899, amid a crowd of onlookers. Its departure was featured on the front page of newspapers all over the world because aboard the ship was a who's who of American conservationists, scientists, and artists. Even today, more than a century away, the names are recognizable—George Bird Grinell, founder of the Audubon Society and the Boone and Crocket Club; John Muir, leading naturalist and father of the conservation movement; and Edward Curtis, one of the most famous photographers of all time.

Harriman's sons Averell and Roland were among the 126 passengers aboard *George W. Elder*. Roland's earliest memory was about the loading of that steamship. Livestock went along on the journey, including a cow brought aboard specifically to provide milk for four-year-old Roland. He remembered seeing a cage of chickens drop from a rope while being swung from the dock and landing in the water between the steamship and the pier. It stuck with him because of his fear for the struggling birds, which were soon saved and dried off to find their home onboard *George W. Elder* where their duty was to supply eggs.

During the 1899 Alaska Expedition, 600 new species were described and entire natural history collections created. The traditions of Alaska's native people were documented and photographed. The Smithsonian published 12 volumes about the trip. It was a grand expedition.

E.H. Harriman purchased the original shares in the Island Park Land and Cattle Company that would become the Railroad Ranch and, eventually, Harriman State Park of Idaho. Harriman made the purchase in 1908 but died before seeing the property. At Harriman's funeral, his friend naturalist John Muir said, "In almost every way he was a man to be admired." Harriman and his sons Averell (left) and E. Roland each ran Union Pacific Railroad in his turn. Harriman's wife, Mary, and their children would often visit the Railroad Ranch after his death. The boys would stay in a log structure called the Boy's House. It has been remodeled to provide meeting space at Harriman State Park of Idaho. Both Harriman boys enjoyed visits to the ranch, but it was Roland who grew to cherish it, taking his family there year after year.

Three

THE RAILROAD RANCH

It was probably not philanthropy E.H. Harriman had in mind when he bought one of five shares in the Island Park Land and Cattle Company in 1908. He probably envisioned hunting and fishing trips in the West with friends and fellow investors. Those trips would never happen for Harriman. He died in 1909, never having seen the ranch.

The Island Park Land and Cattle Company had been organized in 1902 mostly by railroad men associated with the Oregon Shortline Railroad, which was a subsidiary of Union Pacific. E.H. Harriman and his sons Averell and E. Roland each served as president or chairman of the Union Pacific, so at some point people began referring to the 15,000-acre property as the Railroad Ranch.

Both Roland and Averell spent many summers at the ranch, but it was Roland and later his wife, Gladys, who fell in love with the place. Year after year, they would fly in, landing in one of the ranch meadows in their amphibious plane and spending weeks hunting, fishing, and entertaining friends. They also participated in ranching activities, having favorite horses stabled there.

It was a working ranch in that cattle were raised and cared for there and eventually taken to market by rail. There were no tracks at the Railroad Ranch, so they were driven to a nearby siding in Island Park. The harvesting of hay to provide food for the cattle during the harsh Idaho winters was a huge part of the operation.

The ranch did not have to make a profit, so equal care was given to raising cows and to preserving habitat for wildlife. For a time, the ranch also raised elk, even shipping them live to the East where the Harrimans and others could enjoy a taste of the West.

As Roland and Gladys began entering their golden years, they started making plans to preserve the integrity of their beloved ranch. A new Idaho governor would be integral to those plans.

Averell Harriman (front left) and his mother, Mary Williamson Averell Harriman (third from left), are pictured at the dedication of Harriman State Park of New York in 1909. That year, the Harrimans began making regular trips to the ranch property in Idaho E.H. Harriman had purchased shares in. It was known locally as the Railroad Ranch because early investors were associated with the Oregon Short Line, a subsidiary of Union Pacific Railroad. (Courtesy Palisades Interstate Park Commission.)

Although E.H. Harriman, Averell Harriman, and E. Roland Harriman each headed the Union Pacific (UP) Railroad, there was never a spur to the ranch. This picture is of E.H. Harriman's special train in New York, which included the original Arden Car, his personal conveyance. Roland took over the helm of UP in 1946. He had a second Arden Car built for his use in 1950. (Courtesy LC-DIG-ggbain-04220.)

A lot of Hereford cattle were raised on the Railroad Ranch. In this shot from around 1960, Gladys Harriman is on her white horse, Geronimo, and E. Roland is on his horse, Buck. They were taking the herd to the Island Park siding to be shipped to market. (Courtesy Tom Dixon.)

Roland and Gladys Harriman often brought their daughters and their friends along on summer trips to the Railroad Ranch. In this c. 1938 picture, Elizabeth "Betty" Harriman is on her horse, Challis, helping move cattle at the Island Park siding. Her sister Phyllis is on the fence. (Courtesy Tom Dixon.)

Raising cattle year-round at 6,200 feet above sea level calls for harvesting a lot of hay. In the picture above, five sickle bar horse-drawn mowers knock down the hay. The Harrimans bought an early steam tractor for use in the hay harvest but found that it did not work well because of the configuration of the fields and irrigation ditches, so they largely stuck with horse-drawn equipment. In the picture below, several teams are ready to pick up hay with sweep rakes. The horses are harnessed behind the pick-up teeth. In the center is a beaver slide, probably being moved from a finished stack to make a new stack in the field.

There were several variations of the beaver slide, like the one above used at the Railroad Ranch. The purpose of each was to use horsepower—later tractor power—to slide a load of hay up into the air and push it off onto a stack. The woman running the slide is Nona Virgin. Hay was also often loaded by hand onto a wagon, then lifted off onto loose stacks by a derrick, as below. The Railroad Ranch supplied beef to the Army during World War II. After the war, the ranch stopped keeping cattle year-round, so harvesting and stacking hay also ceased.

Cattle were not the only livestock raised on the Railroad Ranch. In the above picture with one of the big barns in the background, elk get their winter feed. A bull Rocky Mountain elk can weigh 700 pounds and stand five feet tall at the shoulder. For a time, they were commercially raised and shipped to markets in the East and sometimes for the Harriman's table in New York. The ranch also tried raising bison commercially, seen below, but found that they were very difficult to keep contained. Note the extra-high fence. Bison were once native to what is called the Island Park area of eastern Idaho, north of Idaho Falls, within which the Railroad Ranch lay.

The Harrimans, particularly Roland and Gladys, frequently visited the ranch, having pilots land their planes in the pasture. The 1938 photograph above shows ranch hands Don Kroker (center) and Harold Hanstead (right) with the Harriman's Grumman Goose parked up against a haystack. The man on the left is an unidentified pilot. Below is the Grumman Goose on a trip to British Columbia in 1938. Roland Harriman and four friends commissioned the first five of these amphibious aircraft, each powered by twin 450-horsepower engines mounted on the leading edge of their wings. The landing gear was hand-cranked into position for field landing. Harriman turned the Grumman Goose over to the Royal Canadian Air Force for the war effort in World War II. It was sold to Central BC Airways and in 1952 crashed and sank during bad weather north of Butedale, British Columbia, with five fatalities. (Both, courtesy Tom Dixon.)

Roland Harriman is pictured on the 1938 trip to British Columbia. The head of Union Pacific for 23 years, Harriman served in several high-level banking positions and was a partner, along with his brother Averell and Prescott Bush, father of Pres. George H.W. Bush, in Brown Brothers Harriman Bank. Roland served as national president of the Red Cross for two terms. (Courtesy Tom Dixon.)

Phyllis Harriman and her sister Betty got their trophies on the trip to British Columbia in 1938. It took the Harriman family two days to fly the Grumman Goose to Edmonton from New York, then a short hop to Deadman's Lake, where supplies awaited them. It had taken three weeks for outfitters to pack those necessities in. (Courtesy Tom Dixon.)

Wealthy or well-placed friends of the Harrimans and other Island Park Land and Cattle Company owners were frequent guests at the Railroad Ranch. Here, Baroness Hilla von Rebay poses with a ranch horse. She was a noted abstract artist in the early 20th century and cofounder and first director of the Solomon R. Guggenheim Museum.

Solomon R. Guggenheim and his brothers Daniel and Morris purchased three cabin lots at the Railroad Ranch in 1906. The brothers sold out to the Harrimans, but Solomon retained his ranch share and properties until his death in 1949. The Guggenheims' wealth came from copper mining. A lifelong collector of art, Solomon is best known for founding what became the Solomon R. Guggenheim Museum in New York City.

Marriner S. Eccles, who was born in Logan, Utah, was a friend of Roland and Averell Harriman and a visitor to the ranch. He was a well-known economist who served as chairman of the Federal Reserve under Pres. Franklin Delano Roosevelt and was a proponent of New Deal programs. The Federal Reserve building in Washington, DC, is named after Eccles.

Charles Jones and his wife, Jenny, built a guesthouse on the property formerly owned by Solomon Guggenheim in 1955. Jones ran Richfield Oil Corporation. The Harrimans purchased Jones's share in 1961. After Charles died in 1970, Jenny donated the furnishings of the house to the State of Idaho.

Famed naturalist John Muir, shown here in a 1902 photograph, went on E.H. Harriman's 1899 Alaska Expedition, along with many other luminaries of the day. Muir maintained a friendship with the Harrimans after the death of E.H. in 1909 and visited the Railroad Ranch in 1913. (Courtesy LC USZ62-52000.)

John Muir visited Mary Harriman and her sons at the ranch in 1913. On Sunday, August 13, 1913, he wrote in his journal: "Arrived Island Park station at 5 or 6 a.m. Got breakfast and (I was) in spring wagon 12 miles to Harriman ranch. Arrived 9 o'clock welcomed by Mrs. H and . . . had a second breakfast."

E. Roland and Gladys Harriman are shown at the Railroad Ranch in the 1930s dressed in typical fashion. They were horse people from the beginning, though their Arden Homestead Stables in Goshen, New York, were not much like the ones at the ranch. The Harrimans were promoters of harness racing and raised trotters at home, including six world champions. E.H. Harriman, Roland's father, was also a trotting fan and owner of two world champions. Roland devoted an entire chapter to the sport in his 1975 autobiography *I Reminisce*. Gladys was the first woman to drive a sulky in under two minutes. Their interests also included breeding and showing English cocker spaniels. Their wealth allowed them to hire full-time trainers and develop their Cinar Kennels in Arden, New York. Gladys was inducted into the English Cocker Spaniel Hall of Fame in 2013. (Courtesy Tom Dixon.)

Steve Bly (left), the second director of the Idaho Department of Parks and Recreation, served during the early years of the period when the Railroad Ranch was transitioning to a state park. In this 1972 photograph, he is with Gladys and Roland Harriman at their cottage looking over plans for the new Harriman State Park of Idaho. (Courtesy Steve Bly.)

IDPR director Steve Bly (left) helps Elliot Richardson show off a trout he caught while visiting the Railroad Ranch in 1974. Richardson was US attorney general during the Nixon administration. He famously resigned rather than fire special prosecutor Archibald Cox on Nixon's order during the Watergate scandal. Richardson also served as secretary of health, education, and welfare and secretary of defense under Nixon, and was secretary of commerce during the Ford administration. (Courtesy Steve Bly.)

Averell Harriman, shown at the ranch in 1937, served as US secretary of commerce under President Truman and later as governor of New York. He twice ran for nomination as the Democratic candidate for president—in 1952 and 1956, defeated by Adlai Stevenson both times. Harriman served as ambassador to the United Kingdom and to the Soviet Union. He is remembered in Idaho as the developer of Sun Valley Ski Resort when he headed Union Pacific.

IDPR director Yvonne Ferrell (left) is pictured with Pamela Harriman during a 1990s visit to the park. Pamela was the third wife of Averell Harriman. She was acquainted with many of the most famous figures of the 20th century, from Adolph Hitler, whom she met as a teenager, to Winston Churchill, who was her father-in-law during her first marriage. Pres. Bill Clinton appointed her ambassador to France in 1993. (Author's photograph.)

Four

HEYBURN STATE PARK
AND THE CCCS

Heyburn State Park came into being in the early days of the state parks movement in the United States. There was no broad consensus of what a state park should be or how one should operate. Funding is always an issue when it comes to operating state parks. In Idaho, an early solution to the funding problem was to lease cabin lots at Heyburn State Park, or "cottage leases" as they are known. Only about 20 acres were set aside for cottage leases out of 6,786 acres of parkland. Over the years, the leases have been a steady source of funding, as well as headaches. Every park that hosts people for overnight stays becomes a quasi village or even a small city, with all the attendant problems people bring with them. Park rangers become the local police, garbage collectors, and town councilors. Beyond those day-to-day interactions, the Heyburn leases once threatened the very existence of the park.

Congress had conveyed the Heyburn property to the State of Idaho with the condition that the property would remain a park and would revert to the federal government if it were not so maintained. The Coeur d'Alene tribe, whose members had historically possessed the site, claimed that leasing cottage sites violated that condition in that allowing private cabins was not a public use of the park. They further maintained that title to the park should revert to the tribe. In 1989, the argument went all the way to the US Supreme Court, which declined to hear an appeal of a Ninth Circuit Court ruling in favor of the State of Idaho.

For the first couple of decades of Heyburn's existence, there was little infrastructure in the park. That all changed when Pres. Franklin Delano Roosevelt took on the Great Depression with a series of new social programs under his New Deal. The Civilian Conservation Corps (CCC) would change the face of the park forever.

STATE OF IDAHO
DEPARTMENT OF PUBLIC WORKS

HEYBURN PARK

RULES AND REGULATIONS

Section 6964 of the Compiled Laws of the State of Idaho provides as follows:

"Any person violating the provisions of any rules or regulations adopted by the owner-ship or management for the orderly and healthful conduct of any park, public ground, dance hall, pleasure or health resort, sanitarium or building, or grounds of any kind or description to which the public has general access, whether owned or operated by the state, a county, a municipality, corporation, association, partnership or individual, shall be guilty of misdemeanor, and upon conviction thereof shall be fined in a sum not less than $10 and not exceeding $100, or imprisonment in the county jail for not less than five days or more than 30 days, or both, in the discretion of the court."

In accordance therewith the Department of Public Works of the State of Idaho has promulgated the following:

RULES AND REGULATIONS:

1. This Park is the property of the State of Idaho and is dedicated to the citizens of Idaho for their use and enjoyment subject to the laws of the state and the rules and regulations provided for the control and government of said Park.

2. All of the laws of the State of Idaho, civil and criminal, shall be applicable to said Park and enforceable within the boundaries thereof, as elsewhere.

3. No portion of the Park shall be occupied by residences, campers, or concessionaries, except by authority of lease entered into with the Department of Public Works.

4. No places of refreshment or entertainment, or bath-houses, launch-houses, boat-liveries, launch-liveries, house-boats, float-houses, bathing facilities, wharves, docks or landings or buildings or structures of any description shall be erected or maintained on the land or waters of the Park without the written authority of the Park superintendent or other authorized agent of the Department of Public Works.

5. No timber, brush, hay, or other vegetation within the Park shall be cut without the written authority of the Park superintendent or other authorized agent of the Department of Public Works.

6. No material shall be removed, excavations made, or buildings, tents, fences, etc., erected on the Park property without written authority of the Park superintendent or other authorized agent of the Department of Public Works.

7. No toilets or other outhouses shall be erected or maintained excepting at the points designated by the Park superintendent.

8. No persons shall scatter or permit to accumulate upon the grounds or in the waters of the Park any offal, refuse, garbage, tin cans, bottles or other containers, but shall make disposition of same as directed by Park superintendent.

9. No springs or other sources of water supply shall be polluted.

10. No fires shall be kindled within the boundaries of the Park except in places designated by the Park superintendent.

11. No signs shall be removed and no trails shall be obstructed within the Park boundaries.

12. Automobiles and other vehicles must be parked in places designated by Park superintendent.

13. Horses or other animals must be tethered in places designated by Park superintendent.

14. All erected tent frames and floors must be taken down and cared for by campers when leaving the camp grounds or otherwise disposed of as directed by Park superintendent.

15. The Park superintendent has full power and authority to enforce all the rules and regulations provided for the use and government of the Park.

BY ORDER OF WM. J. HALL, Commissioner of Public Works

Every park in the Idaho system has a set of rules posted in a prominent place. This rules poster for Heyburn is from 1919. The wording of today's rules varies a bit from these, but they still boil down to "have fun, get along, and leave the park like you found it." US senator Weldon B. Heyburn wanted to create something called Chatcolet National Park. He had some success in the Senate, but the national park bill failed in the House of Representatives. Heyburn State Park was the first major state park created in the Pacific Northwest. Congress set aside 5,500 acres of land and 2,333 acres of water in 1908. Idaho got around to purchasing the property in 1911, for $15,000, using timber taken from the new park as a source for part of the payment.

Tracks that serviced the mines in the Silver Valley cut across Chatcolet Lake on trestles. To allow steamboats to pass through to the St. Joe, the highest navigable river in the world, there was a swinging railroad bridge. The operator in the little house atop the bridge could pivot the whole thing 90 degrees to let the boats pass.

The Trail of the Coeur d'Alenes, jointly operated by IDPR and the Coeur d'Alene tribe, is a 72-mile paved pathway that follows the route of the old railroad. Where it crosses the water in Heyburn, the trail follows the old trestle across the bridge. The bridge no longer swings, though. Engineers raised it high enough above the water to allow sailboats to pass beneath and permanently mounted it in that position.

The Civilian Conservation Corps (CCC) was started in 1933 as one of Pres. Franklin Delano Roosevelt's New Deal programs. It was designed to put young men to work during the Great Depression. In Idaho, there were at least 52 CCC camps. Thirty-five camps were in national forests, six were in state forests, five worked on soil conservation districts, three were on reclamation projects, two served grazing districts, and one was located in Heyburn State Park, where workers made this marker. Many states took advantage of available federal money and the CCC help to create and develop parks. Why Idaho chose to focus on just this single park without creating additional state recreation opportunities is unclear. A reason frequently cited by elected officials over the years for not creating new parks has been the ongoing cost of maintaining them.

The young men of the Civilian Conservation Corps came mostly from local communities, such as St. Maries. They received clothing, room and board, and $30 a month, $25 of which had to be sent home to their families. They got skills training as well, in everything from carpentry to road building.

The CCC members were from 18 to 25 years old, unmarried, and unemployed. In 1935, the age range was extended to 18 to 28. Some were military veterans. Each would sign up for a minimum of six months and could extend for up to two years. They typically worked a 40-hour week, usually five days a week.

Some of what the CCC built at Heyburn goes unnoticed today, simply because it is such an integral part of the infrastructure. The men built park roadways, trails, and a water system. They also hauled in sand for beaches. Upgrades have occurred over the years, but systems they laid out are still in place. (Courtesy ISHS P1987-4-23.)

There was time for fun at the CCC camp at Heyburn State Park. The camp band played for Saturday night dances. The Civilian Conservation Corps was funded year to year by Congress. It was dissolved in 1942 when World War II created another role for the country's young men.

The CCC camps operated under the purview of the Army, so the men always called superiors "sir." They knew that what they were doing was important not just for them, but for their country. Here, the men are doing stonework on what was called an outdoor kitchen in the early days. (Courtesy ISHS P1987-4-24.)

This is the completed kitchen, which serves as a picnic shelter at the park today. The stone masonry of the CCC buildings is a hallmark of their construction. Doing this work gave the men a sense of self-worth. Decades later, most of the CCC men looked back on their experiences with great pride.

At a CCC reunion, park staff learned that the crude structure in this tree was left over from CCC days. It was a fire lookout. Unlike more formal lookouts in forests today, this one was a platform where someone could stand and take a regular look around for smoke after climbing up the tree.

Over the years, many Civilian Conservation Corps men came back to Heyburn State Park to reminisce. From left to right are Fred Blood, Andy Hightower, Ray Wozny, Rex Wendle, Swede Hansen, Kent Hart, and Walt Stallmen at the dedication of a plaque honoring the CCC in 1993. They are standing in front of the lodge at the park, one of several CCC buildings.

Five

THE CATALDO MISSION OF THE SACRED HEART

Every fourth grader in Idaho learns about the Cataldo Mission of the Sacred Heart during his or her Idaho history sessions. It is the state's oldest building.

In 1740, Chief Circling Raven had a great vision that foretold of men with long black robes and crossed sticks. He told his people to watch for them. Over 100 years later, this prophecy would be fulfilled. Delegations of Salish-speaking people traveled to St. Louis to request Fr. Peter De Smet, SJ, build missions in the Rocky Mountain West.

Father De Smet, a Jesuit priest born in Belgium in 1801, met with members of the Coeur d'Alene tribe in 1842, and the first log mission was built. Subsequent flooding caused it to be abandoned. After moving to the current site in 1846, construction of the new mission began in 1850 and was completed in 1853. It was Fr. Anthony Ravalli, SJ, an Italian-born priest, who designed and directed the building of the mission. The priests, brothers, and some 400 tribal members had only simple tools such as a whipsaw, broadaxe, augur, ropes and pulleys, and a penknife.

A stone foundation holds up 30-foot-high walls made of mud, grass, and willow saplings interlaced in what is called wattle-and-daub construction. Tall wooden pillars and columns are held together by wooden pegs. No nails were used in the original construction. The building was clad with clapboard in 1865, hiding the inner walls, but park visitors can still see exposed sections on the interior, complete with fingerprints of those who worked on them. The flooring for the mission, the steps, and the iconic columns marking its entrance were cut from local pines. The columns were shaped by hand with a broadaxe to a fine finish.

Father Ravalli showed his skill on the finer interior appointments as well. He and others carved three altars, decorating each with paint to resemble marble, and fashioned chandeliers from tin cans. Ravalli patiently carved statues of the Blessed Virgin Mary and St. John the Evangelist from blocks of white pine with a penknife.

This 1884 photograph of Cataldo Mission was taken by Fr. Jay Haynes more than 30 years after its completion. Even this early in its history, the building is showing some wear, particularly on the entrance steps where several members of the Coeur d'Alene tribe are standing. The mission would fall into disrepair and be brought back several times. Now managed as a state park, the building's upkeep is routine.

Mission Landing was a transportation hub on the Coeur d'Alene River a short distance from Cataldo Mission of the Sacred Heart. Steamboats, like the *Georgie Oakes*, ran between here and Coeur d'Alene. For years, it served passengers while a railroad line brought ore out of the Silver Valley mines. The mission sits on a hill overlooking the landing.

The distinctive baroque facade of the Cataldo Mission of the Sacred Heart has changed little over the years with the ebb and flow of restoration. It underwent major repairs in 1884, 1910, and 1929. This shot from the mid-1920s shows it with two urns on the steps of the facade. Later restorations included the four urns of the original design.

This 1958 photograph from the National Park Service's Historic American Buildings Survey shows the interior of the mission, much of the detail of which was done by Anthony Ravalli. He carved statues with a penknife, painted faux marble finishes, and constructed chandeliers from tin cans. (Courtesy LC HABS ID,28-CATAL.V,1—11.)

Renovation and repair of the mission has taken place many times over the years. This 1958 picture shows children Janet Regan and Larry Edson in front of a concrete truck involved in work on the entrance. They are likely children of caretakers. The mission had a series of on-site caretakers over the years until IDPR took over management in 1975.

In 1961, Interior Secretary Steward Udall designated the mission a National Historic Landmark. In 1975, it underwent a major restoration as part of the nation's bicentennial celebration. The adjacent parish house was rebuilt after a fire in 1887 and underwent a restoration in the 1990s. It contains many artifacts used in daily life by the priests at the mission. (Idaho Heritage Trust photograph.)

Fred Walters, an expert in historical architecture from Idaho Heritage Trust, has worked with Coeur d'Alenes Old Mission State Park several times in the past to advise on restorations. In this 2016 photograph, he is documenting columns and pilasters. Replacing the hand-split cedar shingles on the roof of the building was next on the restoration list.

Most of the columns that grace the front of the mission are original, though one was partially replaced in 2006. In 2016, the National Park Service (NPS) Ebby's Landing restoration crew did more work on the column bases. Here, Jason Benson, left, from NPS is detailing a replacement wood block while Lanny Neipert of IDPR assesses a column base corner for a new Dutch joint.

The watercolor of the mission (above) was done in 1854 by John Mix Stanley. It was turned into a lithograph published in the *Pacific Railroad Report*, vol. 12. The reports, commissioned by the secretary of war, are detailed examinations seeking the most practicable and economical route for a railroad stretching from the Mississippi River to the Pacific Ocean. In 2013, assistant US Capitol curator Amy Burton discovered that the watercolor was the inspiration for one of the paintings done by Constantino Brumidi for the Senate wing of the Capitol. In the Brumidi fresco (below), the mission becomes a nondescript building on a hill. Still, there is good evidence this representation is the only one of the frescos that depicts a building that is still standing. (Below, courtesy LC DIG-thc-5a37675.)

Six

FARRAGUT NAVAL TRAINING STATION

The attack on Pearl Harbor on December 7, 1941, taught the Navy about the vulnerability of facilities. The site for the new Farragut Naval Training Station (FNTS) was selected because it was far inland yet located on the shores of Idaho's largest and deepest lake, Lake Pend Oreille. The site was chosen in March 1942. By September of that year, the first recruits arrived. Pres. Franklin D. Roosevelt visited the new base on September 21, 1942.

FNTS consisted of five training camps—Bennion, Ward, Waldron, Hill, and Scott—and two camps, Peterson and Gilmore, housed special schools. All the camps were named after naval heroes killed in the line of duty. The naval station itself was named for Adm. David Glasgow Farragut, the first admiral in the US Navy.

At full capacity, FNTS housed 45,000, making it the second-largest "city" in Idaho. It was eventually the transient home of 293,381 recruits, or "boots" as they were called.

The second-largest training station at its time, FNTS operated only for 26 months. Of the 776 buildings constructed for the war effort, only a handful remain today, mostly in the form of small utility buildings such as a pump house. The brig is the most significant remnant of FNTS, probably because it was made from concrete. Most buildings were constructed of timber, not all of it well cured. The structures were meant for short-term service in the war effort.

After the war, some of the buildings became the site of Farragut College and Technical Institute. That closed in the spring of 1949 due to lack of funding and low enrollment.

Farragut Naval Training Station (FNTS) encompassed 4,050 acres on the southern end of Lake Pend Oreille. It is Idaho's largest lake at 148 square miles and deepest at 1,150 feet. This aerial, taken around 1943, shows the completed training site. The ovals near the center of the picture are the training camps with buildings surrounding drill fields.

This photograph shows construction at Camp Waldron barracks in 1942. Construction at FNTS began in March, and recruits started training in September of the same year. The final construction budget was $57 million. Recruits, called "boots," would train there for only 26 months. Even so, 293,380 recruits received their basic training here.

New recruits would arrive in civilian clothing and soon find themselves in a barber chair (above). The barbers in this picture are, from left to right, M.C. Garcia, L.J. Perillo, L.M. Alameda, L.S. Burns, J. Nemeth, F.R. Thomas, H. Duvall, R.L. Cline, and S. Orozco. A regulation cut was a maximum of three inches on top. After their trim, the boots got inoculations, medical and dental exams, and were fitted for uniforms (below), all within 90 minutes. They would receive $133 worth of personal belongings, which included a mattress, hammock, and blanket. Their next stop would be their assigned barracks, which would be home for 6 to 13 weeks depending on whether they attended one of the special schools on base.

Each barracks held two companies of recruits, one topside and one on the lower deck. Signs reminded the men that the ceiling was now the overhead, the floor was the deck, and the front was the bow. This barracks is ready for one of the regular living quarters inspections. Blankets had to be taut and clean, seabags tied just so, and their contents spotless and meticulously folded.

Each of the training camps had drill fields called "grinders" where the recruits marched. The huge regimental drill hall in the background allowed training during all kinds of weather. The drill halls were said to be the largest clear span (without posts) structures in the world at that time. This particular structure is believed to be the drill hall at Camp Bennion.

It was no accident that FNTS was located on the shores of a big lake. The recruits were training for naval duty. They had to be able swim 75 yards, and each spent hours in all weather conditions in 16-man steel whaleboats on Lake Pend Oreille. Each company picked its best rowers for team competitions in training session championships. This is Camp Bennion Company 3043 in June 1944.

During rifle training, 100 men at a time could fire their rifles on the FNTS range. The men soon learned to hold their 30.06 rifles tight against their shoulders to avoid the jolting recoil. During the peak of training, about 12,000 rounds of ammunition were fired every day. Both the lead and the brass were salvaged and recycled into new ammunition.

Ship-to-ship and ship-to-station communication was often done by flag semaphore when radio communication was risky. By the time recruits were headed to sea, they knew the semaphore alphabet from A to Z. To help them learn the flag positions for each letter, the alphabet was painted on the walls of their barracks. Here, a cartoon character helps remind the boots about the need to learn semaphore. Also on the wall above men reading the FNTS newspaper is a cartoon encouraging them to learn how to quickly don a gas mask. Murals giving short instructional reminders were common all around the base.

The weekly *Farragut News* was the essential form of communication for the boots on station. Here, Hugh Lago (right), yeoman third class, briefs a work detail ready to deliver the paper announcing the naming of Camp Gilmore, which opened on June 26, 1944. The newspaper first came out December 12, 1942, and the final edition rolled off the presses on June 13, 1946.

Communicating with the folks back home was also essential. Most recruits wrote letters about their experiences at Farragut Naval Training Station, but they had another option. The Navy had a recording studio set up so that the men could share their thoughts and their voices with their families or that girl who was waiting.

Boots visited the ship's stores often to stock up on necessities such as paper, envelopes, pencils, and postage. Because of the training station's remote location, finding local men and women to help staff the stores and do other work on the base was difficult. The ship's stores gave the men the opportunity to buy books, cigarettes, magazines, sunglasses, candy, snacks, and personal care items for themselves. For those waiting anxiously to hear from them at home, the sailors could purchase jewelry, stuffed animals, and other souvenir-related items. One popular gift item for women was the "sweetheart" pillow. Covered in sateen and bordered in fringe, there were versions for mothers as well as sweethearts.

Sandpoint, Idaho, photographer Ross Hall provided class photographs the boots could buy. The photographs included a list of those pictured. The picture above is Company B, 11th Battalion, Third Regiment. Its commander was F.J. Bischoff, chief specialist. Many such photographs are on file today at Farragut State Park to help those wanting to know more about family members who went through training at FNTS. Below, three "Ross Hall Girls," who kept track of names of those in the pictures, are shown in their booths with a class lined up for a photograph in the background. In March 1944, a record 20,891 boots had their pictures taken.

One little-known aspect of FNTS is that it served as a prisoner-of-war camp. More than 200 German POWs arrived at the station in February 1945. They were interned at the Butler Overflow Area, where the Butler Construction Company, which built the base, had its administrative offices. The prisoners were guarded by Army troops while there. Perhaps as many as 926 POWs spent time at Farragut, clearing brush and shoveling coal mostly, but also as bakers, cooks, storekeepers, and firefighters. They even had their own newspaper (below). Long after the war, a former prisoner would occasionally show up at Farragut State Park for a visit. They generally had good memories of their time there.

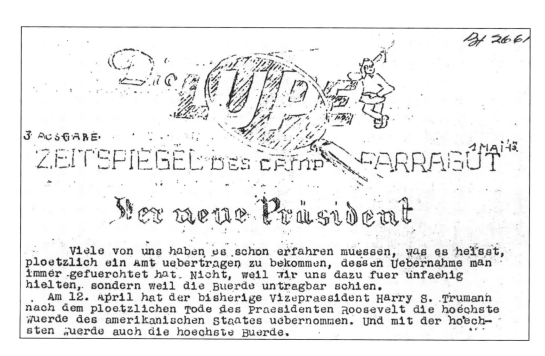

Seven

THE FATHER OF IDAHO'S STATE PARKS

Robert E. Smylie ran for governor of Idaho in 1954 at least partly to create a system of state parks for the enjoyment of citizens and to encourage economic development through tourism, according to his autobiography *Governor Smylie Remembers*. He talked often during his campaign of reorganizing Idaho's natural resource agencies and putting an emphasis on attracting tourists.

One of Smylie's first acts as governor was to commission a survey of the state's natural resources. He chose Leon G. Green, head of the Department of Health, Physical Education, and Recreation at the University of Idaho, to conduct the survey and make recommendations for "a comprehensive overall plan" for the "preservation and development" of those resources.

In 1959, Smylie called for the creation of a Department of Natural Resources, consolidating existing agencies and containing a new division of state parks. The Idaho Legislature ignored his suggestion.

Smylie trimmed down his proposal for a natural resources agency for the next legislative session, asking instead for only a state parks agency. The bill narrowly passed the House but died in a Senate committee.

Then an opportunity came along that Smylie was quick to recognize. The governor had known E. Roland Harriman for some time when, in 1959, the co-owner of the Railroad Ranch called. Harriman and his brother Averell wanted to see the land they owned protected from development by donating it to the State of Idaho.

Governor Smylie saw this as his chance to create a park system. Working mostly with Roland Harriman, the majority owner, Smylie inserted language in the gift deed that Idaho would be required to have a professionally trained park service in place before the transfer of the property was made.

Even with the donation of the Railroad Ranch as a tempting carrot, the 1963 legislature refused Smylie his state parks department. Finally, in 1965, with the help of a newly minted federal program that would provide substantial capital for development of a park system and a contract with the Girl Scouts for a big event in north Idaho in hand, lawmakers gave the governor what he wanted.

Lucile Irwin met Robert Smylie while she was working as a secretary for a law firm in Washington, DC. Smylie was going to law school at George Washington and was working as a law clerk at the same firm. When World War II came along, Smylie enlisted in the Coast Guard and was stationed in Philadelphia. He made a trip to Washington, DC, to propose marriage. Lucille accepted, but she had also accepted a posting with the State Department in Brazil. That kept them apart for a time, but in December 1943, upon her return, they were married in New York City. Smylie was stationed for a short time in the Philippines just as the war was ending. Jobs were scarce at the DC law firm after the war, so Smylie accepted a position as assistant attorney general to the newly elected Idaho attorney general, Robert Ailshie. (Courtesy Robert E. Smylie Archives, College of Idaho.)

Robert E. Smylie was appointed to the office of attorney general in Idaho in 1947 when Robert Ailshie died in office after serving only a few months. Smylie was elected to a full term in 1950, then was elected governor in 1954. Smylie was one of five Idaho governors born in Iowa. He first came to the state in 1934 to live with an aunt and uncle while attending the College of Idaho in Caldwell. Smylie would get a degree from the Idaho school, then go on to George Washington University Law School, where he would graduate in 1942. He and his wife, Lucille, had two boys. This picture was taken at their cabin. Their younger son, Bill, is on the left, with Steve next to him. (Courtesy Robert E. Smylie Archives, College of Idaho.)

Gov. Robert E. Smylie thought that Idaho's lackadaisical management of state parks could be improved if a corps of professionals were put in charge. He promoted his idea for a state parks department in State of the State speeches before the Idaho Legislature in 1959, 1961, 1963, and finally 1965. The legislature met biannually at the time. In 1958, as chair of the land board, Smylie pressed to hire John W. Emmert, a retired former superintendent of Glacier National Park, to oversee a new division of parks in the Idaho Department of Lands. The job was only part-time, but it marked the first time anyone had set out to plan a direction for an Idaho system of state parks. (Courtesy Robert E. Smylie Archives, College of Idaho.)

The first Idaho Park Board poses with the governor in June 1965. From left to right are (sitting) W.M. Frome, St. Anthony; E. Hedlund, St. Maries; and Beth Durham, Lewiston; (standing) J.C. Sandberg, Blackfoot; Harold Brown, Filer; Gov. Robert E. Smylie; and Ernest Day, Boise. (*Idaho Statesman* photograph.)

In 1966, the Ada County Fish and Game League presented Governor Smylie (right) with an award for effectiveness in leadership, recognizing him for creating the state parks department, among other achievements. Presenting the award to Smylie is Ernest Day, a Boise real estate developer and conservationist who also served on the Idaho Park Board. (*Idaho Statesman* photograph.)

In 1964, Governor Smylie was promoting Idaho at a meeting of New York executives put together by E. Roland Harriman. Harriman had earlier joked, "One gripe I have abut Idaho is that in 53 years of residence, I've never been permitted to buy a resident fishing license. I've never lived there three months at a time. The result is that I have to buy a nonresident license. But I only have to stay there six weeks to qualify to get rid of my spouse. There's something screwy about a state that thinks more of a fish than a spouse!" Smylie took the opportunity to present Harriman with a badge making him an honorary deputy officer of the Idaho Fish and Game Department. In a letter thanking Smylie for the honor, Harriman writes, "Gladys was not a bit impressed with the badge and identification card you gave me. She said it would have been much more effective if she had been made the official as she is much more hardboiled than I am." (Courtesy Robert E. Smylie Archives, College of Idaho.)

Eight

THE SCOUTS HELP CREATE A PARK SYSTEM

Gov. Robert E. Smylie helped sell the idea of creating a state park system in Idaho by landing a series of three important Scouting events at Farragut State Park. Smylie considered the acquisition of Farragut from the federal government key in his quest to create an agency to manage state parks in Idaho. Getting an agreement from the Girl Scouts to bring in nearly 10,000 girls and leaders for the 1965 Girl Scout Roundup made acquisition of the site irresistible to legislators. The state traded state lands being inundated by the planned Dworshak Dam for the old Farragut Naval Training Station site.

It took just 21 weeks of feverish wartime work to carve a naval training station out of the forested lands on the southern end of Lake Pend Oreille in 1942. It would take two years and $2 million to remove the concrete and other remnants of the base to get Farragut ready to host the Girl Scout Roundup of 1965.

Just as the Girl Scouts were wrapping up their roundup, Smylie announced that he had also secured the 1967 World Boy Scout Jamboree for Farragut State Park. It would be the first World Scout Jamboree to be held in the United States. At the time this book was written, it remained the only one hosted in the United States.

For the World Scout Jamboree, the state developed a swimming beach, a water system, an amphitheater that could hold 60,000, and a new headquarters building for the park. But the Scouts were not finished leaving their mark on Idaho. The state also landed the National Scout Jamborees in 1969 and again in 1973. The latter was a joint jamboree shared with Moraine State Park in Pennsylvania.

Girl Scouting
A PROMISE IN ACTION
Girl Scout Senior Roundup   Farragut, Idaho   July 15-28, 1965

The idea for inviting the Girl Scouts to Idaho came from Jayne Brown of McCall. The energy and drive to make it happen came from Governor Smylie. Finding $2 million in the state budget back in 1963 was not easy. Smylie convinced state leaders to take $750,000 from the Permanent Building Fund, and he got the Idaho National Guard and reserve engineers to dedicate training time to demolition and construction at the old Farragut Naval Training Station. Guard units from Boise, Idaho Falls, Nampa, and Ashton spent two summers ripping down most of the remaining buildings, plowing under the concrete and steel foundations, and removing those asphalt marching fields called "grinders" that had served so many boots. In place of that, they planted bluegrass, rye, sweet clover, and wildflowers. Smylie named Maj. Gen. John Walsh, Idaho adjutant general, as his special assistant. The two would personally oversee the state's part in the event in July 1965. The newly formed Idaho Department of Parks would not begin management of Farragut until September of that year.

The 1,700 Girl Scout staff members and volunteers, most of them from New York City, quickly learned they were a little west of Park Avenue. They were fascinated by the nearby Nez Perce teepee encampment. Encountering a deer—not at all uncommon at Farragut—was startling. Here, they are starting to do some set up for the roundup.

For the staff and volunteers, their trip to the "wilderness" started at New York City Army-Navy stores, where, according to public relations assistant Mina Wetzig, they "bought shiny black boots and khaki colored rain coats, duffel bags, and ponchos." When they arrived at Farragut, they found tents already set up but little else. Each got an orange crate to use as a dressing table and a galvanized pail for water.

Margaret Price, national president of the Girl Scouts of America, poses with some Girl Scouts at the 1965 Girl Scout Roundup. Price and Governor Smylie cut a ribbon at the intersection of streets named Price Road and Smylie Boulevard to open the event. Smylie Boulevard is still the name of the main road through Farragut today.

Winnie Ambrose (left) of Meridian, president of the Gem Area Girl Scouts Council, and Louise Shadduck, secretary of Commerce and Development for the State of Idaho, talk about the selection of Farragut as the site for the 1965 International Senior Girl Scout Roundup. (*Idaho Statesman* photograph.)

Kathy McShane of Nampa (left) hosted Japanese Girl Scouts Yasuko Niiyama (middle) and Tomoko Yasurawa (right) prior to the Girl Scout Roundup at Farragut State Park. Governor Robert E. Smylie had invited the girls to Idaho. (*Idaho Statesman* photograph.)

One hundred twenty-seven flags of national pride and celebration flew over the encampment, including flags from 68 nations and 50 states. No sooner had they gone up than they were ordered lowered to half-staff to honor Adlai E. Stevenson, the US ambassador to the United Nations who died of a heart attack in London on July 14. They remained at half-staff until after his funeral.

During the opening ceremonies, Lucille Smylie looked out over the crowd of girls and said, "Really, you know I've got a lump in my throat and goose pimples are going up my back." The governor shouted over the noise, "If you want a comparison in numbers, there are as many people here on this Idaho spot right now as live in Caldwell." The program opened with 11,000 voices singing Girl Scout songs, recordings of which still sell occasionally on eBay today. Margaret Price addressed the girls as the national Girl Scout president. She said, "The federal government, the government of Idaho and the Girl Scout councils have invested much in you. Equal to our nation's faith in you (are) our expectations of you."

Just two days after the Girl Scout Roundup concluded, Governor Smylie sent out a press release announcing that Farragut had been selected as the site for the World Scout Jamboree. Governor Smylie, right, said, "Idaho is bigger today. The biggest planned event in Idaho's history is no longer a hope; it's an assured occurrence. And I'm sharing the lift in pride and pleasure enjoyed by all Idahoans when I say that the invitation I was privileged to extend in the state's name, has been accepted by the Boy Scout World Jamboree." Below, Governor Smylie samples an Idaho baked potato during the 1966 US and Canadian Latter-day Saints (LDS) Scout Encampment held at Farragut State Park. (Both, courtesy Robert E. Smylie Archives, College of Idaho.)

Polished Idaho jasper stones are being pasted on cards for distribution during the World Scout Jamboree as souvenirs by, from left to right, Boise Scouts Tom Love, Bob Hallock, and Max Christensen as Gov. Don Samuelson looks on. The three Scouts represented Boise at the jamboree. Hallock would, years later, serve on the RV Advisory Board of the Idaho Department of Parks and Recreation. (*Idaho Statesman* photograph.)

Flags of 108 nations were raised over Farragut State Park on August 1, 1967, to mark the beginning of the first World Scout Jamboree to be held in the United States. The theme for the nine-day jamboree was "For Friendship," while the musical theme was the Disneyland attraction song "It's a Small World (After All)," which was originally written for a UNICEF exhibit at the 1964–1965 New York World's Fair.

An icebreaker wide game kept Scouts busy early in the jamboree. Each was given a letter, and they were charged with finding Scouts from other places with the remaining letters that would make up the word "friendship." The goal was to get Scouts of several nations together. This photograph, in front of the World Scout Jamboree sign, shows one successful group.

Calls to home from the jamboree were popular, so the phone company installed temporary phone booths for the Scouts. If one dialed 208-BSU-1967, one got the switchboard for the World Scout Jamboree, which could then get a message to a Scout. Estimates were that more than 100,000 calls were made by attendees.

The Skill-O-Rama at the jamboree was where Scouts could watch dancing, listen to music, and taste the foods of other lands. They could also practice their own skills at everything from scuba diving to gold panning, with a little limbo thrown in. A contingent of seven Scouts and two leaders from Haiti was the first to check in, arriving on July 28, 1967. Scouts from Thailand, the Netherlands, Germany, and Guatemala were close behind. A German Scoutmaster pedaled 4,500 miles from Guatemala on his bicycle to get to the jamboree. In all, 108 nations were represented at the World Scout Jamboree. The site was divided into 10 subcamps, each named for a previous host nation. At the time this book was written, the gathering at Farragut was the only World Scout Jamboree ever held in the United States.

Astronaut Scott Carpenter was at the jamboree, along with the original *Aurora 7* capsule from the Mercury space program, in which he orbited the earth in 1962. Carpenter also served as a swimming, archery, and hiking coach for several days during the event.

The year 1967 marked the Diamond Jubilee for Scouting, celebrating the first outing of founder Sir Robert Baden-Powell. Powell died in 1941, but his widow, Lady Olave Baden-Powell, chief guide of the World Girl Scouts, was an honored guest at the World Scout Jamboree, which she called "the United Nations in action."

Celebrity sightings were common at the World Scout Jamboree. Vice Pres. Humbert Humphrey was there. So was Jimmy Stewart (in hat). It was not Stewart's first trip to Idaho. He was a flight instructor and squadron commander in the 29th Bombardment Group at Gowen Field in Boise during World War II.

The Idaho Land Board approved cutting trees to make 20,000 poles of varying lengths for the jamboree. They would be used for temporary fencing, flagpoles, skills events, and a permanent marker to commemorate the event. There were 400 US flags and 400 troop flags. Additionally, small flags flew from each of the estimated 20,000 tents. Some logs were used in a log throw competition.

Idaho Statesman staff writer David Zarkin explained one important linguistic difference to readers: "The British and Scottish youths are unanimous in their praise for the American "birds." A casual observer should not mistake this remark for an interest in ornithology. These European lads are expressing their pleasure in being on the receiving end of the hospitality extended by the teen-aged Spokane girls (birds) during a dance preceding the jamboree."

Pres. Lyndon B. Johnson declared August 1–9 Boy Scout Week, saying he hoped the World Scout Jamboree would "quicken among boys of many nations the desire for understanding and passion of peace upon which rests the future of all men." Rumors flew during the event that the president might drop in at any minute. Alas, when the minutes ticked their last, he had not made an appearance.

The most significant investment at Farragut for the World Scout Jamboree was the nearly $200,000 for development of the beach and the 500-person swimming area at Beaver Bay, which included construction of a bathhouse, restrooms, and a 140-car parking lot. A permanent water system was installed, as was a 60,000-person amphitheater and a new park headquarters building.

Scouts from all over the world were greeted by a smoke-belching insect called a guberif, courtesy of the Idaho Department of Lands. For years, the agency had been stenciling "Don't be a Guberif" on highways all over the state. It was meant to make people ask the question, "What's a guberif?" It was actually firebug spelled backwards. The theory was that it would stick in the mind better than "don't start fires."

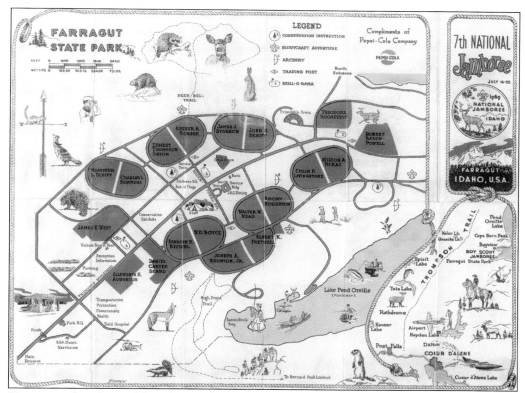

Two years after the world jamboree, the Scouts were back at Farragut, this time for a national jamboree. This map shows the layout of the event, but it also shows the historic footprint of Farragut Naval Training Station. Note the oval camp areas named for various Scouting officials. Those correspond to the training camps from the days of the Farragut boots.

The national jamboree was big news in Idaho, but it was not what the nation was paying attention to. A UPI story on July 17, datelined Farragut State Parks, reports: "At 7:32 a.m. Wednesday Apollo 11 lifted off for its trip to the moon. Two hours and 21 minutes later the Seventh National Scout Jamboree blasted off for its week-long journey to adventure for the 35,000 scouts and leaders gathered here."

Some Scouts biked to the 1969 jamboree, though probably not on a Stingray. A fleet of 100 Air Force transport planes brought the Scouts to Idaho, each plane making as many as three trips a day, adding up to 67 extra landings and departures daily. On the highways, 300 charter buses delivered Scouts, along with 182 shuttle buses running back and forth between the Spokane airport and Farragut. (*Idaho Statesman* photograph.)

Chopping wood for campfires was out, though there were some demonstrations involving wood. A Scout spokesman said, "We can't have 40,000 boys running around chopping down trees and denuding the area." Charcoal briquettes and mechanical fire starters were the solution, though the spokesman hastened to add that all the Scouts attending jamboree had passed their woodlore tests. (*Idaho Statesman* photograph.)

Keeping the 34,251 Scouts healthy was a top priority. The Idaho Department of Health caught chipmunks in the park and spent a little time combing them for fleas. The fleas were then tested to assure there was no sign of plague or tularemia, a rare infectious disease that can be transmitted to humans. The fleas came up clean, and the chipmunks were released. Rodent grooming was not the only thing on the list for the Idaho Department of Health. For eight months prior to the jamboree, they checked food and food sources that would be used. Water tests were performed daily, each one coming up clean. (*Idaho Statesman* photographs.)

Sen. Frank Church attended the final ceremonies. Astronaut Col. Frank Borman delivered a message from President Nixon on the closing night of the jamboree and presented a film from Neil Armstrong's first step on the moon, which had occurred a few days before. Only a handful of Scouts had seen the televised event, so the entire crowd sat spellbound watching the scene from the moon and hearing Armstrong's words. Both Borman and Armstrong were former Scouts. Armstrong acknowledged the Scouts from space on his way to the moon, saying "Hello to my fellow Scouts and Scouters at Farragut National Park in Idaho." No one attempted to tell Commander Armstrong (pictured) that it was actually a state park. He went on to say, "They're having their national jamboree down there and I'd like to present our best wishes." (NASA photograph.)

Nine

PARKS LOST, PARKS FOUND, PARKS THAT NEVER WERE

The term *state park* was used loosely over the years, sometimes referring to an 8,000-acre jewel such as Heyburn State Park and other times a roadside rest with a picnic table and trash can. Not until 1965, when the Idaho Department of Parks came into being, did standards begin to apply. Roughly stated, a state park now had to be of statewide significance. Though it is a stretch to call some sites even in the current system of statewide significance, all are far removed from roadside picnic stops.

Many small properties transferred from the Department of Lands when the parks agency was created. Deep Creek Park, Sunnyside Park, Land Board Park, Bogus Basin Recreational Area, Ward Massacre Monument, American Falls Boat Dock, Aberdeen Sportsman Park, Seagull Bay, and Hagerman Refuge were declared excess to the needs of the agency by the Idaho Park and Recreation Board in 1972, leaving the decision of what to do with those parks to the land board.

It is impossible to assure a comprehensive list of park proposals over the years, as some got little attention at all. In the years since statehood, the following sites have been proposed as state parks: Tubbs Hill in Coeur d'Alene, Shoshone Ice Caves, Horsethief Reservoir, Civil Defense Caves near Ashton, Craters of the Moon, Redfish Lake, Boise Barracks, Wolverine Canyon, Fort Lemhi, and Lava Hot Springs.

Additionally, several sites were state parks and no longer are, including Indian Rocks south of McAmmon, Veterans Memorial in Boise, Spalding homesite, Canoe Camp, Shoshone Falls, Packer John's Cabin, Hagerman Fossil Beds, Hammett, Pine Creek, Mann Creek, Black Canyon, and C.A. Robbins State Park near Arco. Mores Creek, Robie Creek, Chimney Rock, Barclay Bay, and Turner Gulch—all sites around Lucky Peak Reservoir—once operated as state parks or state park units but are now managed by the US Army Corps of Engineers.

A handful of other properties owned by the Idaho Department of Parks and Recreation may become state parks one day or may be traded for property more readily developable.

The federal government deeded Lava Hot Springs to the State of Idaho in 1902, which gives it some claim of being Idaho's first state park. However, the legislature did not officially name it a state park until 1912. Created by statute in 1962, the Lava Hot Springs Foundation consists of a five-member board appointed by the governor. (Courtesy ISHS 78-37-10.)

Proposals to set aside some of the Boise Front as a state park started as early as 1917, when 2,000 citizens petitioned the Boise City Council to support a resolution to that effect. This photograph was taken in the 1940s. Bogus Basin was one of the holdings transferred to the Idaho Department of Parks in 1965; it returned to the Department of Lands in 1972. (Courtesy ISHS 1992-30-134-83.)

In 1918, the Thomas family, above, enjoys a camping trip at Billingsley Creek, near Hagerman. The two family members identified in this photograph are the children—Bob Thomas (on the left in the light-colored stocking cap) and his brother Eldred Thomas (on the right). Billingsley Creek would become a unit of Thousand Springs State Park in 2002. In the 1980s and 1990s, the Thomas brothers would serve the Idaho Department of Parks and Recreation—Bob as an Idaho Park and Recreation Board member and Eldred as a member of the RV Advisory committee. Below, Bob, who also served Idaho as a fish and game commissioner, is still wearing a stocking cap in this self-portrait at Farragut State Park around 2000.

Mormon settlers started a little community near Salmon in 1855, calling it Fort Limhi, after King Limhi, an important figure in their religion. Over the years, the spelling changed to Lemhi, and the name stuck, attached now to the Lemhi Valley, Lemhi County, and Lemhi River. The settlement itself lasted only about three years. It was abandoned after relations with the Shoshone Nation deteriorated. In 1917, L.W. Shurtleff of Ogden, Utah, one of the original residents of Fort Lemhi,

This is a view of Boise Barracks, probably from the 1880s. The military left the fort in 1912. In 1948, Congress proposed to dispose of 26 old military forts at bargain prices to be used as parks. Boise Barracks, the site of the military's Fort Boise, was to be sold to the State of Idaho for $42,000

spoke to the Idaho House of Representatives, advocating for a state park to be built at the site of the abandoned settlement. In 1940, former Idaho secretary of state Ira H. Masters proposed a state park there, envisioning a reconstruction of the stockade. In 1970, the Idaho Department of Parks considered the site. Nothing came of any of the proposals. (Courtesy ISHS 166E.)

for use as a state park. However, it was the City of Boise that ultimately acquired the site in 1950, developing Fort Boise Park and Community Center. (Courtesy ISHS 77-180-2c.)

Land Board State Park was dedicated in 1953. The two-acre grove of old-growth cedar trees was set aside by the Idaho State Land Board to honor—wait for it—Idaho State Land Board members. The photograph at left, taken in 2005, shows Heyburn State Park manager Fred Bear in front of the largest tree, named after Gov. Len B. Jordan. Signs on other trees name the larger ones for Ira Masters, then secretary of state; Alton B. Jones, then superintendent of public instruction; Arthur Wilson, a former legislator and land board commissioner; and attorney general Robert E. Smylie. Below is Smylie with his tree in 1953, probably at the site's dedication. IDPR has never managed the site, though it still carries the moniker of state park on some maps. (Below, courtesy Robert E. Smylie Archives, College of Idaho.)

In 1921, Prof. O.J. Smith of the College of Idaho gave a presentation to the Caldwell Kiwanis Club extolling the virtues of a place he called "Valley of the Moon," near Arco. He promoted the idea of making the site a state park. Smith was not the only one who was excited about the lava fields. Robert Limbert, an Idaho promoter who was often called "Two-Gun Bob" because of his trick-shooting shows, was on a mission to tell the world about the Valley of the Moon. He and a friend had explored the rugged area in the spring of 1920, taking many pictures. By 1924, Limbert had convinced *National Geographic* magazine to run an extensive article he had written about his adventure. He also sent the president a scrapbook of pictures. Within two months, Pres. Calvin Coolidge issued a proclamation establishing Craters of the Moon National Monument. In this picture, an unidentified man examines the imprint of a fallen tree in the lava. (Courtesy ISHS 76-2.5a.)

PACKER JOHN'S CABIN
ONE FOURTH MILE NORTH BUILT 1862
FIRST DEMOCRATIC TERRITORIAL
CONVENTION HELD IN CABIN FALL OF 1863
ERECTED BY SONS AND DAUGHTERS
OF IDAHO PIONEERS 1936

Packer John's Cabin, near New Meadows, was the site of the 1863 Idaho Democratic Party Convention and the 1864 Republican Party Convention. Today, it seems like an odd location for important political events, but at that time, there were only four counties organized in the state—Shoshone, Nez Perce, Idaho, and Boise. Given that geographic distribution, the little cabin was somewhat centrally located. A 1985 photograph (above) shows a replica of the cabin, which no longer exists. The site of Packer John's Cabin was designated a state park in 1935. In 1936, the Meadows Post No. 111 of the American Legion and the Sons and Daughters of Idaho pooled their resources to place a $100 marker (left) next to the highway at the entrance to the tiny park. The site was deeded to Adams County in 1992 and is now a county park.

This 1874 photograph by Timothy H. O'Sullivan shows why it is no surprise that Shoshone Falls was proposed as Idaho's first state park in 1891, when the *Idaho Statesman* editorialized about the potential for a "grand state park" there. The state, only a year old then, was barely out of diapers and ill-equipped to develop anything for public recreation. (Courtesy LC-DIG-ppmsca-10072.)

There was a movement to make the falls a national park, but Gov. Frank Steunenberg—who would later be assassinated after leaving office—requested that the federal government abandon plans for a Shoshone Falls National Park. He was afraid such a designation would negatively impact Twin Falls Land and Water Company's ambitious plans for an irrigation system in the Magic Valley. (Courtesy ISHS 71-115-18.)

It was not until 1909 that the legislature named Shoshone Falls a state park. A Senator Sweeley, who proposed the bill, said, "The land is rough and rocky and so cut by the Snake River and ravines as to be of practically no financial value, but with the proper outlay and attention can be developed into an asset of great importance to the state."

This 1910 photograph shows a private hotel that operated on the site for a time, built by Charles Walgamott in hopes of getting the property through adverse possession. A survey proved that he did not actually own the land where it was built; the State of Idaho did. (Courtesy ISHS 73-221-786.)

In this 1920 picture by Clarence E. Bisbee, Mr. and Mrs. Lind are in the front seat of a Buick. Mrs. Alot and the Linds' two daughters—Helen, left, and Lilly, right—are in the back. In 1932, the City of Twin Falls received a donation of land near the falls, and in 1933, the state turned over its operation to the city, which manages the site today. (Courtesy ISHS 73-221-26.)

Often misidentified as a state park, this gravity-defying hoodoo has a 17.5-inch base holding up a 40-foot-wide table of rock. Websites and maps persistently call it a state park, though it is on property managed by the Bureau of Land Management. Balanced Rock Park, an interesting little canyon that is nearby, is not a state park either. It is managed by Twin Falls County Parks and Recreation. (Author's photograph.)

Henry (left) and Eliza Spalding, accompanied by Marcus and Narcissa Whitman, set out to open Presbyterian missions in the Pacific Northwest. The Whitmans established their mission near the Walla Walla River in what is now Washington State. The Spaldings chose a spot two miles up Lapwai Creek in Idaho. They moved their mission in 1838 to a site overlooking the Clearwater River about 11 miles east of present-day Lewiston. The Spaldings shared their message with the Nez Perce until 1848. They abandoned their mission when the Whitmans and 11 others were killed by members of the Cayuse tribe, who blamed them for a deadly outbreak of measles. The marker below commemorates the Spalding Mission Site. (Below, courtesy ISHS 42.)

This c. 1935 photograph shows the Joe Evans Museum. The building was constructed by the federal government in the late 1850s as part of the Indian agency. The Idaho House passed a bill in 1941 to purchase the building and its Indian artifacts. The bill died in the Senate. The owners sold the contents to the State of Washington. (Courtesy Nez Perce National Historical Park, NEPE-HI-0082.)

Spalding became a state park in 1936. Canoe Camp, shown in this c. 1963 photograph, was a part of the park. It was where Lewis and Clark's Corps of Discovery carved out five canoes for the last leg of its trip. Idaho managed the park until 1966, when the National Park Service took over, incorporating the site into the newly designated Nez Perce National Historic Park. (Courtesy Nez Perce National Historical Park, NEPE-HI-0913.)

TO THE MEMORY OF
THE PIONEERS WHO WERE
MASSACRED BY INDIANS
NEAR THIS SPOT
AUGUST 20, 1854.

THIS MONUMENT IS DEDICATED
BY
PIONEER CHAPTER

DAUGHTERS   OF THE
AMERICAN   REVOLUTION

BOISE   IDAHO

WILLIAM WARD   AGE 44
MARGARET WARD   " 37
MARY WARD   " 13
ROBERT WARD   " 16
EDWARD WARD   " 7
FRANCIS WARD   " 2
FLORA WARD   " 5
SUSAN WARD   " 3
ELIZA WHITE   " 30
GEORGE WHITE   " 4
SAMUEL MALLAGAN
CHARLES ADAMS
WILLIAM BABCOCK
DR. ADAMS
——— AMEN
ADOLPH SCHULTZ
JOHN FREDERICK
FRENCH CANADIAN

The legislature created Ward Massacre State Park in 1953. IDPR turned many small properties, including this half-acre site, back to the Idaho Department of Lands in 1972. Some websites still list these long-forsaken properties as state parks, though they are often no longer even state property. This small park, between Middleton and Caldwell, is now managed by Canyon County Parks and Recreation. The memorial, placed there by the Pioneer Chapter of the Daughters of the Revolution, commemorates an Indian attack on a 20-member party on its way to Oregon in 1854. Only two boys survived. Military retaliation for the attack so enraged the Indians that Hudson's Bay Company posts at Fort Boise and Fort Hall had to be abandoned and travel on the Oregon Trail without military escort became unsafe. (Courtesy ISHS 595.)

In this 1968 photograph, Bob Romig, curator of collections, examines the skeletal remains of a small, zebra-like horse from the Hagerman Fossil Beds. The Smithsonian Institution collected 15 similar skeletons in the 1930s. Interest in the fossil site led to interest in it becoming a state park. IDPR managed the site for several years before turning it over to the National Park Service in the 1990s. (*Idaho Statesman* photograph.)

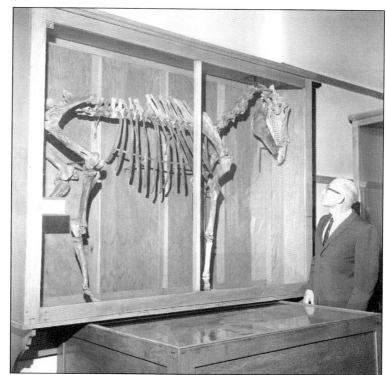

Veterans Memorial State Park was created in 1982 on the site of the Old Soldier's Home on State Street in Boise. The park memorializes war veterans, hosts numerous related ceremonies, and serves as a quiet park along the Boise River and Greenbelt. IDPR turned operations over to the City of Boise in 1997 through a long-term lease. The 81-acre park is now named simply Veterans Park.

IDPR acquired 3,000 acres south of Pocatello from the US Bureau of Land Management in 1968 through the Federal Recreation and Public Purposes Act for $2.50 an acre. The Indian Rocks State Park visitor center, above, was located on the west side of I-15 at the exit to Lava Hot Springs. Park planners hoped campers would stop on their way to Yellowstone National Park. They also hoped a planned reservoir nearby would attract boaters and fishermen. The US Army Corps of Engineers decided there was not enough public support for building a reservoir on nearby Marsh Creek. The park closed in 1983 during a state budget crisis, and it never reopened. That there are only two pictures of the park in existence, including the restroom photograph below, is a good measure of the park's popularity while it was open.

Ten

IDAHO'S STATE PARKS
YESTERDAY AND TODAY

The Idaho Department of Parks and Recreation celebrated its 50th anniversary in 2015. The system of parks Governor Smylie envisioned back in the 1950s exists today as 30 state parks, serving about four million visitors a year. Smylie's wisdom regarding the economic impact of state parks proved true. His foresight also turned out to be the savior of the system he created.

In 2010, during the Great Recession, Gov. Butch Otter recommended defunding the Idaho Department of Parks and Recreation, effectively eliminating it. Opposition from legislators and citizens was strong, but another factor played into the decision to drop that proposal. The language Gov. Robert E. Smylie had inserted in the Harriman gift deed in 1961 was strong enough to give attorneys pause when the elimination of the department was under consideration. If the Harriman gift was predicated on the existence of a professional agency being in place to operate parks in Idaho, it could mean the state would be obligated to return the property to Harriman heirs. The loss itself would be substantial, but it would also start a cascade of demands for the return of money granted to the state since 1965 through the Land and Water Conservation Fund. The State of Idaho used the donation of the Railroad Ranch as a match when applying for development and acquisition funds at other state parks, including Farragut and Eagle Island. Eliminating the agency could eventually save money, but it could cost many millions to achieve that savings.

That scare in 2010 encouraged citizens to form a watchdog group that would be in place in case another threat to Idaho's state parks should appear. That organization is the nonprofit sponsor of this book, the Friends of Idaho State Parks. Those who appreciate their parks are encouraged to join the group by going to its website, www.idahofriends.org.

Massacre Rocks, sometimes called "Gate of Death" or "Devil's Gate," was a narrow choke point along the Oregon Trail where travelers passed between lava outcrops. The formation got its name because of fears of ambush. It was actually about two miles west of the rocks where a wagon train was ambushed in 1862. Travelers in five wagons clashed with Shoshone Indians from August 9 to August 12, 1862, resulting in 10 immigrant deaths. Col. Patrick Conner and his troops retaliated for this and other skirmishes in January 1863 by attacking a Shoshone winter camp along the Bear River, killing as many as many as 490 men, women, and children. That event is known today as the Bear River Massacre. The photograph above shows the old highway going through in the 1940s. Below, I-86 follows the Oregon Trail through the substantially widened gap today.

Massacre Rocks was a well-known point for travelers along the Oregon Trail and along Highway 91-191 in later years. In this picture from the 1940s, one can see the motel that existed just to the east of the formation. It was still there, though abandoned, in 1969 when the landmark became Massacre Rocks State Park.

Another wagon train came through Massacre Rocks in 1976. It was the Bicentennial Wagon Train retracing the Oregon Trail. Though the park got its name from the rocks, it is boating and fishing on Snake River, a 42-unit campground, and camper cabins that attract visitors today. More than 200 species of birds have been identified in the park, which is along a major flyway.

Oregon Trail pioneers carved their names in a big rock just west of present-day American Falls, as seen in this photograph from the 1940s. It was among the highway department's roadside rest areas for years and often referred to as Register Rock State Park. It actually gained that status but lost its name in 1965 when the Idaho Legislature created Massacre Rocks State Park, which includes the Register Rock unit.

The McLane family enjoys Robbie Creek in 1956, a year before it became a state park. Dennis McLane, in the water, would later work for California state parks and retire as the deputy chief of law enforcement for the Bureau of Land Management. In his retirement, he serves on the board of directors of Friends of Idaho State Parks. (Courtesy Dennis McLane.)

The construction of Lucky Peak Dam, above, in the 1950s created Lucky Peak Reservoir. The Idaho Department of Parks managed several recreation sites around the reservoir, including Robie Creek, Chimney Rock, Barclay Bay, Turner Gulch, and Mores Creek in the 1960s, but turned many of them back over to the US Army Corps of Engineers to manage in the 1970s. Sandy Point, Spring Shores, and Discovery are all units of what is now Lucky Peak State Park. Spring Shores, which is now Spring Shores Marina, was a popular site for boating, fishing, and hanging out on the beach back in the 1960s when this picture was taken. (Above, courtesy Morrison Knudsen Corporation collection, Boise State University Library, Special Collections and Archives.)

Virgil McCroskey's parents homesteaded near Steptoe Butte, about eight miles from Colfax, Washington. He was a pharmacist by trade and a conservationist by heart. McCroskey purchased Steptoe Butte, below, a place where he had played in his youth, and turned it over to the State of Washington in 1945. His gift became Steptoe Butte State Park. In 1939, he started purchasing land in Idaho along the ridgetops north of Moscow, overlooking the patchwork fields of the rolling Palouse Prairie, with the idea of preserving that as an Idaho state park. To his surprise, he met resistance from the Idaho Legislature when he tried to give the state the property he had acquired.

When Virgil McCroskey approached the Idaho Legislature in 1951 about accepting his gift of land, legislators worried about upkeep and about taking 2,000 acres off the property tax rolls. Friends formed the Skyline Drive Association to lobby the Idaho Legislature. McCroskey himself purchased more property to add to the gift. By 1954, he had 4,400 acres to offer and a new governor, Robert E. Smylie, as a supporter. Still, the legislators were concerned about maintenance, so McCroskey, 79 years old, agreed to maintain it himself for the next 15 years. The lawmakers agreed, and McCroskey kept his word, taking care of the site until just before his death at age 94 in 1970. In a sense, he still cares for the park today. McCroskey left $45,000 in trust to the state to be used for maintenance of Mary Minerva McCroskey State Park. At the 1955 dedication of the park, Virgil McCroskey is holding Elaine McCroskey with Craig Sartwell standing next to him. They were great-grandchildren of Mary Minerva McCroskey, for whom the park is named.

Idahoans are seldom quick to embrace cutting-edge societal trends. "Idaho's Woodstock" came along two years after the real thing. But it was the fame and infamy of that iconic music festival that caused the imaginations of many Idahoans to soar with hope or trepidation in the summer of 1971. The younger generation, in their teens and twenties, hoped for big-name bands like Iron Butterfly, Santana, and Grand Funk Railroad. The generation that had passed the age of 30, that famous barrier to trustworthiness at the time, envisioned drugged-out hippies by the thousands and the moral calamity of free love. The event did not live up to the imagination of either group. This poster advertising the picnic belongs to former Idaho Park and Recreation Board chair Steve Klatt of Sandpoint. He attended the picnic and was lucky enough to find and save one of the posters, which were created by R. Crumb of "Keep on Truckin'" fame. (Courtesy Steve Klatt.)

In May 1971, organizers filed a form with Farragut State Park for a "church picnic attended by at least 200 people." That probably seemed inconsequential to park manager John Grieg. Farragut had hosted nearly 35,000 people for six days just two years earlier, during the National Scout Jamboree. It soon became obvious these folks were not Boy Scouts. (Courtesy Steve Klatt.)

Word reached local law enforcement personnel that hippies were about to descend. They quickly asked the Idaho Department of Parks to deny the seemingly innocuous permit. As parks officials dithered, north Idaho leaders asked the governor to intervene. Gov. Cecil D. Andrus said that since all the concerns expressed were purely speculative, he had no reason to deny a church from meeting on state land. (Courtesy Steve Klatt.)

The bands that played were a who's who of who's that? Cadillac, Annakonda, Survival, Celebration, Greenfield Morning, and Sidartha were some of the bands that day. When it was all over, park manager Greig was quoted as saying, "As far as I'm concerned, they can have one of these every weekend, all summer. The picnickers left the park cleaner than the Boy Scouts did and we can really use all the money it collects at the entrance." (Courtesy Steve Klatt.)

There were no arrests made at the 1971 Universal Life Church Picnic. Park rangers at the entrance charge a $2 camping fee and collected dollar bills in paper bags from some 15,000 attendees. A little skinny dipping and open use of marijuana were noted by the *Spokesman Review*. Meanwhile, the Universal Life Church was offering free minster's licenses at the event, just as they do today online. (Courtesy Steve Klatt.)

Not everyone in Idaho was as pleased with the picnic as the park manager was. A self-appointed committee lead by Stanley D. Crow of Nampa dissects every detail of the picnic in a document called "The Farragut report: A study of the Universal Life Church picnic held at Farragut State Park and recommendations for legislative and administrative action." (Courtesy Steve Klatt.)

The event, if not the report, inoculated the agency for 40 years against rock concerts at Farragut State Park. The 65,000-person amphitheater originally built for the World Scout Jamboree, along with available parking for hundreds of cars, would have made Farragut State Park a logical site for stadium-sized concerts serving Spokane, Coeur d'Alene, and other points in the Pacific Northwest. Agency officials have shown little enthusiasm for another concert, though. (Courtesy Steve Klatt.)

Boise State University professor Tom Trusky added much to the history of Idaho's state parks by "rediscovering" filmmaker Nell Shipman. Shipman had a film studio at Lionhead Lodge on the north end of Priest Lake, where today's Lionhead Unit of Priest Lake State Park is located. Trusky searched for lost copies of Shipman's films all over the world, finding prints in Canada, England, and Russia.

Because of the scholarship of Professor Trusky, who passed away in 2009, Boise State University is the home to a digital collection of Shipman photographs and other memorabilia. Trusky edited the 1987 Shipman biography, irresistibly titled *The Talking Screen and My Silent Heart*. Many of her films are available online. Revival of interest in Shipman resulted in an award-winning 2015 documentary called *Girl From God's Country*, by Boise filmmaker Karen Day. (Courtesy Photographic Services Collection, Boise State University Library, Special Collections and Archives, Nell Shipman Collection.)

Tom Trusky wrote the following in 2008 for an IDPR history book: "In the summer of 1922, Nell Shipman Productions moved from Spokane, Washington to its final residence, Priest Lake, in the Panhandle of north Idaho. There, the company would complete shooting of what historians and silent film fans term Shipman's magnum opus, *The Grub-Stake* (1922), and four noteworthy two-reel films in a series titled *The Little Dramas of the Big Places* (1924). Although Shipman, her lover Bert Van Tuyle, her 10-year-old son Barry (by her first husband, Canadian film entrepreneur Ernest Shipman), and her crew could not have known it, this was sundown for the democratic, 'Indie,' one-girl-do-it-all days of cinema. Dawn of the next day, the studio system and male movie moguls would define for decades what Hollywood meant, prior to the advent of television, Gloria Steinem, Sundance, satellite feeds, and on-line downloads." (Courtesy Photographic Services Collection, Boise State University Library, Special Collections and Archives, Nell Shipman Collection.)

Shipman was a pioneer in treating animals humanely in her movies. This is a barge loaded with her menagerie on Priest Lake around 1922, headed for Lionhead Lodge, her film studio at the north end of the lake. Looking closely, one might see Brownie bear in silhouette in the cage at the front of the barge. Brownie appears in several of her movies, often with Shipman's son Barry. (Courtesy Photographic Services Collection, Boise State University Library, Special Collections and Archives, Nell Shipman Collection.)

Nell Shipman was the screenwriter, director, star, and stunt woman in her movies. They feature strong women more likely to save men from danger than the other way around. Her pioneering included what by today's standards would be a PG-rated nude scene of her showering beneath a waterfall. The movie was hyped with the slogan, "Is the nude, rude?" Shipman Point in Priest Lake State Park is named for this early film pioneer. (Courtesy Photographic Services Collection, Boise State University Library, Special Collections and Archives, Nell Shipman Collection.)

This is what the famous Thousand Springs, near Hagerman, looked like about 1905. The photographer was probably standing on what is now called Ritter Island, which today is part of Thousand Springs State Park. Most of the water has been captured for power production and aquaculture, giving a much-diminished view of the springs. Minnie Miller Springs is the largest remnant that can still be seen today. (Courtesy ISHS 69-4.219/B.)

This photograph of boaters on Payette Lake is from about 1900. Efforts to turn most of the state-owned property around the lake into a state park sputtered along from about this time until 1957, when Ponderosa State Park was finally created. It is one of the most popular parks in the system today. (Courtesy ISHS 1267.)

While Idaho's leaders went back and forth about what to do with state land around Payette Lake, the Idaho Department of Lands leased some of it to private interests who built a community of rental structures such as those above, called Lakeview Village. Newspaper advertisements, like the one below from the July 14, 1944, edition of the *Idaho Statesman*, lured visitors to a beautiful spot where park headquarters sits today. Most of Ponderosa State Park sits on the peninsula that juts out into Payette Lake, where nearly 1,000 acres offer visitors camping, biking, boating, and nature trails. At the north end of the lake, another 500 acres at North Beach beckon swimmers and paddlers. North Beach is where much of the 1940 film *Northwest Passage*, starring Spencer Tracy, Robert Young, and Walter Brennan, was filmed.

This 1939 photograph shows the islands in the upper center that give this famous Oregon Trail crossing its name. Immigrants had to decide whether they would stay on the south side of the river, to the left, which offered a shorter but more difficult route, or cross for better livestock feed and more potable water. About half risked the crossing. Many casualties are recounted in pioneer diaries. (Courtesy ISHS 69-130.2.)

Three Island Crossing State Park today features a modern campground and the Oregon Trail Interpretive Center on the outskirts of Glenns Ferry. Three former governors and then governor Dirk Kempthorne were at the dedication of the interpretive center in 2001. Former governors are, from left to right, John Evans; Cecil D. Andrus, who also served as secretary of the interior; and Phil Batt.

When Timothy H. O'Sullivan took this picture in 1868 for the US Geological Exploration of the Fortieth Parallel, he listed it as Sphynx Rock. California Trail pioneers and just about everyone else since refer to this formation as the Twin Sisters. It is part of City of Rocks National Reserve, which has been jointly managed by the Idaho Department of Parks and Recreation and the National Park Service since 1988. (Courtesy LC-DIG-ppmsca-11931.)

Just a few minutes away from City of Rocks National Reserve is Castle Rock State Park, just on the Idaho side of the border with Utah. The sites share the same headquarters building in Almo. Castle Rocks became a state park in 2003. Both parks attract rock climbers from all over the world.

In this photograph from about 1970, Gov. Don Samuleson and Idaho Department of Parks and Recreation director Wilhelm Beckert discuss Idaho's Statewide Comprehensive Outdoor Recreation Plan, production of which every five years is a requirement for participation in the federal Land and Water Conservation Fund Program. Beckert was the agency's first permanent director.

Fashions have changed a bit since this picture of swimmers and boaters was taken at Bear Lake in 1910. Bear Lake State Park is in the extreme southeast corner of Idaho. About half the lake is in Idaho and half in Utah. The better beach is at the north end of the lake; so many swimmers and boaters from Idaho and Utah spend summer days there. (Courtesy ISHS 72-189-136A.)

Land of the Yankee Fork State Park was selected as Idaho's Centennial Park in 1990. From left to right are park manager Rick Brown, Idaho Park and Recreation Board chair Glenn Shewmaker, director Yvonne Ferrell, and Joint Finance and Appropriations Committee cochairs Kitty Gurnsey and Atwell Perry. They are cutting the ribbon at the dedication of the Challis interpretive center for the park in 1992.

Land of the Yankee Fork State Park focuses on the history of mining in central Idaho. Visitors can see the ghost towns of Custer, Bonanza, and Bayhorse, as well as the Yankee Fork Dredge, charcoal kilns, and pioneer cemeteries. This photograph of the Charles A. Pfeiffer house was taken in the 1890s. This is probably Charles and Ellen Pfeiffer and their family. Pfeiffer ran the general store in Custer. (Courtesy ISHS 73-215.11.)

Members of an unidentified family pose at the top of the big dune at Bruneau Dunes State Park in the mid-1960s. The 4,800-acre park offers camping, hiking, fishing, and horseback riding. One can also slide down the dunes on a rental board or stay after dark to watch the stars in the observatory.

Upper Mesa Falls, at 114 feet, and nearby Lower Mesa Falls are the last major waterfalls on the Snake River that flow unimpeded. Though not technically a state park, the visitor center and grounds around Upper Mesa Falls are managed by Harriman State Park, under an agreement with the US Forest Service.

Winchester Lake State Park was created in 1968. The park belongs to the Idaho Department of Fish and Game, but it is managed by the Idaho Department of Parks and Recreation through an agreement. It features a secluded campground, several rental yurts, hiking trails, and many fishing piers. The nearby Wolf Education and Research Center, operated by the Nez Perce tribe, is a major attraction.

This is the gracefully arched footbridge that takes hikers across an arm of the lake at Winchester Lake State Park. Local lore says that Winchester was named in a public meeting when citizens decided to name the town based on which rifle more citizens had—Remington or Winchester.

In 1969, park manager Jerry Hover shows off a new sign map that illustrates where the trails and campgrounds are in Ponderosa State Park, near McCall. Hover was employed by the Idaho Department of Parks and Recreation for several years but retired as the director of Kansas Department of Wildlife and Parks.

Sandy Point swimming area at the foot of Lucky Peak Dam is a unit of Lucky Peak State Park. In this late 1960s photograph, swimmers frolic while water shoots out in a plume from the toe of the dam. Seattle City Light added power-generating turbines to the dam in 1988, eliminating the plume. It still shoots occasionally when water is routed away from the turbines for maintenance. (*Idaho Statesman* photograph.)

In 1970, IDPR purchased land on both sides of Malad Gorge to create Malad Gorge State Park, near the town of Bliss. In this picture, park manager Rick Cummins poses on the canyon rim. The I-84 bridge is in the background, and the waterfall into Devil's Washbowl is below that. A footbridge was later installed across the gorge so that visitors could access both sides of the canyon. In later years, Malad Gorge would become a park unit of Thousand Springs State Park, which also includes Niagara Springs, Crystal Springs, Billingsley Creek, Box Canyon, and Ritter Island units. All of the sites are associated with the Snake River as it passes through Idaho's Magic Valley region and contain views of various springs. The aquafer below the Snake River Plain acted like a sponge, soaking in water over the centuries. That water pours out from the canyon walls in the Magic Valley through the fissured lava.

Idaho Department of Parks and Recreation director Steve Bly (left), Gov. Cecil D. Andrus (center), and Boise mayor Dick Eardly look over plans in 1974 for what would become Veterans Memorial State Park. Bly, the agency's second director, would later work for Washington State Parks and the Boise Visitor and Convention Bureau before starting a career as a professional travel photographer.

Dale Christiansen, IDPR's third director, was the director of parks for the City of Portland before coming to Idaho. In this c. 1980 photograph, he and Gov. John Evans pose in the governor's office. One of the major park accomplishments during Evans's 10 years as governor was the development of camping and picnicking facilities at Bear Lake State Park using the Idaho National Guard for much of the engineering and construction.

The 1935 winter photograph above shows the family home that came with the property the Idaho Department of Parks and Recreation purchased around Round Lake in 1973. The house was renovated to serve as a park visitor center, below. Round Lake is a 143-acre park near Sagle, Idaho. By Idaho standards, it is a small park, offering nonmotorized boating, camping, hiking, and swimming in the summer, with ice fishing, ice skating, and cross-country skiing in the winter. It offers a camping atmosphere much like people remember it from 1950s, with the campground loop occupied by smaller camping units and tents and lots of campfires in evidence.

There have been hundreds of people who played a role in the development of Idaho's state parks over the years. Here are some on a planning retreat around 1974. From left to right are (first row) development bureau chief Merl Mews, director Steve Bly, administrative assistant Ruthy Kassens, and deputy director Phil Peterson; (second row) planner Lowen Schuett, operations chief Bill Dokken, and planner Kent Ellis.

This is an aerial of a feature even few IDPR employees know about. It is a landform sculpture of an eagle seen as Eagle Island State Park was being developed in 1982. It is still in place today but difficult to distinguish. The park was the site of the old Idaho State Prison Honor Farm, near the city of Eagle.

This picture from about 1971 shows a picnic shelter at Hells Gate State Park on the outskirts of Lewiston. The park was developed by the US Army Corps of Engineers and turned over to IDPR that year. In the left of the picture above, just above the hood of the car, one can make out a large pedestal. That is a sprinkler gun with a 1.5-inch nozzle. It, and others like it, were effective in watering the park grass until the trees grew to be 25 feet tall. The big sprinkler guns are mostly gone now. Below, the park was one of the stops for the Wally Byam Airstream event that gathered in Boise in 1986.

Idaho celebrated its centennial in 1990. The creation of Land of the Yankee Fork State Park was one of the state's major centennial projects. To bring awareness of the celebration, a new centennial license plate was created and this balloon with the centennial logo traveled around the state. Here it is at Hells Gate State Park in 1990.

Bruneau Dunes State Park is home to the tallest single-structured sand dune in North America, at 472 feet. The park was created in 1967. This photograph, from the mid-1980s, was taken by IDPR's second director, Steve Bly. By that time, he was well into his career as an award-winning travel photographer. (Courtesy Steve Bly.)

In the 1880s, Arthur and Mary Hallock Foote lived in the house on the right-hand bank of the Boise River, seen in this photograph. They kept livestock just across the river on the point of land at left. The river meander has changed somewhat, but the Discovery Unit of Lucky Peak State Park is today located just across the river on that point. Discovery is so called because it was at about this point where the Wilson Price Hunt Party was said to have first seen the Boise River. Arthur was an engineer who designed the canal system in the Boise area, and Mary was a well-known author and illustrator in her day. A fictionalized version of their life became the 1972 Pulitzer Prize–winning novel *Angle of Repose* by Wallace Stegner. (Courtesy ISHS 228.)

In the 1930s, the men of the Civilian Conservation Corps were working all over the state of Idaho. They worked in only one state park, Heyburn. In 1999, IDPR took over management of another site where the CCC did some work for the Bureau of Reclamation. The rock wall in the center of this aerial photograph at Lake Walcott State Park was a CCC project.

Gov. Cecil D. Andrus (left), IDPR director Yvonne S. Ferrell (center), and Idaho Park and Recreation Board chair Monte Later plant a western white pine in front of the new IDPR headquarters during the dedication of the building in June 1994. The western white pine is Idaho's state tree.

People are often surprised to learn that IDPR does not own all Idaho state parks. Parks owned by other entities—Bureau of Reclamation, US Army Corps of Engineers, and Department of Fish and Game—but managed by IDPR include parts of Farragut, Land of the Yankee Fork, Thousand Springs, Bear Lake, City of Rocks, and Lucky Peak and all of Dworshak, Hells Gate, Winchester Lake, Lake Walcott, and Lake Cascade (pictured).

Dworshak State Park is one of many owned by a federal agency but managed as a state park. The US Army Corps of Engineers owns the property and constructed most of the facilities before turning everything over to IDPR to manage. Pictured are park manager Mike McElhatton (left) and Gov. Cecil D. Andrus with the dedication plaque for the park in 1989.

This is the view of Henrys Lake State Park from atop Sawtell Peak in 1989. Henrys Lake is Idaho's only seasonal park. Heavy snows at the 6,470-foot elevation make winter access impractical. Note that park names such as Henrys Lake do not contain a possessive apostrophe, in compliance with naming conventions of the US Board on Geographic Names.

The Ashton to Tetonia Trail, managed by IDPR, follows an abandoned railway line in eastern Idaho. Unlike northern Idaho's Trail of the Coeur d'Alenes, this 29.6-mile trail is not paved. Bikers and hikers here will find a gravel pathway. The trail, which is open to snowmobiling in the winter, crosses several trestles, including the 300-foot-high Bitch Creek Trestle shown here.

The Coeur d'Alene Parkway is a 5.7-mile paved path that lies along the north shore of Lake Coeur d'Alene. It is part of the North Idaho Centennial Trail that meanders 24 miles from the Idaho-Washington state line. Higgins Point, at the eastern end of the trail, is a hiking and picnic area popular in the winter for eagle watching.

Ernie Day served on the Idaho parks board from 1965 through 1969 and again from 1976 to 1988. He may have served Idaho best when he resigned in protest to Governor Samuelson's endorsement of a mining company's application to build a road into the White Cloud Mountains in 1969. It was a pivotal moment in the long fight to protect the area. Congress finally created the White Clouds Wilderness area in 2015.

DISCOVER THOUSANDS OF LOCAL HISTORY BOOKS FEATURING MILLIONS OF VINTAGE IMAGES

Arcadia Publishing, the leading local history publisher in the United States, is committed to making history accessible and meaningful through publishing books that celebrate and preserve the heritage of America's people and places.

Find more books like this at
www.arcadiapublishing.com

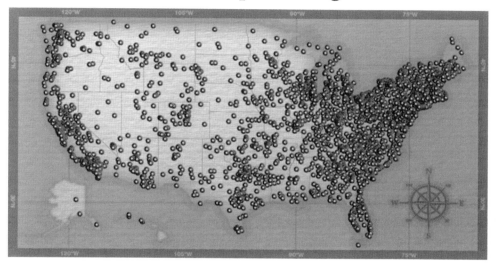

Search for your hometown history, your old stomping grounds, and even your favorite sports team.

Consistent with our mission to preserve history on a local level, this book was printed in South Carolina on American-made paper and manufactured entirely in the United States. Products carrying the accredited Forest Stewardship Council (FSC) label are printed on 100 percent FSC-certified paper.

MADE IN THE

Gov. Dirk Kempthorne's Experience Idaho initiative in 2006 resulted in upgrades to several parks, including a new master plan for Eagle Island, where this picture was taken. From left to right are administrative director Dave Ricks, operations director Dean Sangrey, director Bob Meinen, Kempthorne, communication manager Jennifer Okerlund, planning chief (and author of this book) Rick Just, and Idaho Park and Recreation Board chair Ernie Lombard. Kempthorne would be named interior secretary that same year.

Governor Smylie is at the opening of the new Idaho Department of Parks and Recreation headquarters building in 1994. On September 18, 1998, Gov. Phil Batt presided over the ceremony naming it the Robert E. Smylie Building. Governor Smylie, the father of Idaho state parks, passed away in 2004.